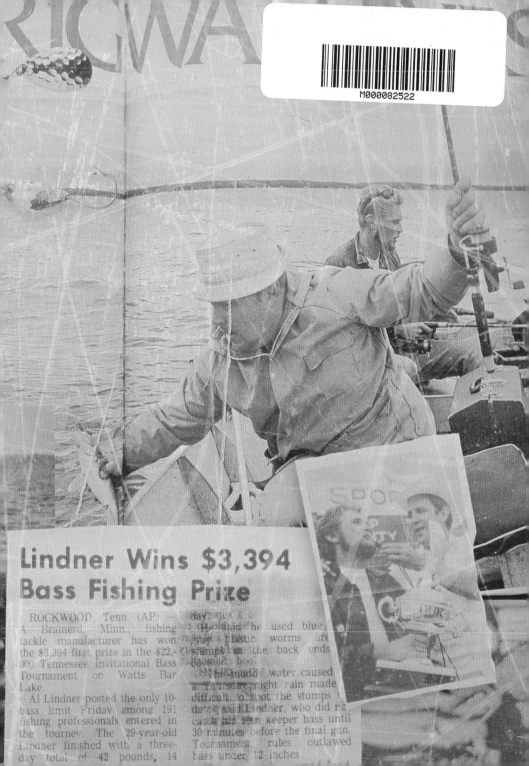

Lindner Wins $3,394
Bass Fishing Prize

ROCKWOOD, Tenn. (AP) — A Brainerd, Minn., fishing tackle manufacturer has won the $3,394 first prize in the $22,000 Tennessee Invitational Bass Tournament on Watts Bar Lake.

Al Lindner posted the only 10-bass limit Friday among 191 fishing professionals entered in the tourney. The 29-year-old Lindner finished with a three-day total of 42 pounds, 14

day, he said, he used blue plastic worms around stumps in the back ends of several coves.

The muddy water caused by Thursday night rain made difficult to spot the stumps, said Lindner, who did not catch his first keeper bass until 30 minutes before the final gun. Tournament rules outlawed bass under 12 inches

Al Lindner

Enjoy and God Bless.

PRESENTED TO

_____

BY

_____

LINDNER'S
Angling Edge
Network

FirstLight
ON THE WATER

Al & Ron
Lindner

Strength
& Honor

BRONZE
BOW PUB

First Light
ON THE WATER

Photography: Bill Lindner Photography, 2617 E. Hennepin Ave., Mpls., MN 55413
        www.blpstudio.com

For information regarding the "Lindner's Angling Edge" and "Lindner's Fishing Edge" television shows, check out the website at: www.anglingedge.com.

ISBN 1-932458-02-6

Published by Bronze Bow Publishing, Inc., 2600 East 26th St., Minneapolis, MN 55406. You can reach us on the internet at: www.bronzebowpublishing.com

Literary development and design: Koechel Peterson & Associates, Mpls., MN 55406
        www.koechelpeterson.com

Manufactured in Hong Kong.

Table of Contents

Al & Ron Lindner

WITH LONG CAREERS SPANNING THE MOST REVOLUTIONARY YEARS IN SPORT FISHING HISTORY, Al and Ron have become renowned industry leaders. They are co-founders of Lindy Tackle as well as In-Fisherman, Inc., both of which have since been sold. With its numerous radio and television shows and magazines, In-Fisherman has become North America's largest multimedia sport fishing network. Together Ron and Al have developed a comprehensive lake, river, and reservoir identification classification system, a fish response calendar, and the famed $F + L + P = S$ (Fish + Location + Presentation = Success) formula, which has been described as the algebra of angling.

Al is hailed as one of the world's best all-around anglers. He was first inducted into and later enshrined in the National Freshwater Fishing Hall of Fame. Besides being one of the earliest partici-pants in professional major bass tournaments in the South and a two-time Bassmaster Tournament

There he stands, draped in more equipment than a telephone lineman, trying to outwit an organism with a brain no bigger than a bread-crumb, and getting licked in the process.

PAUL O'NEILL

winner and qualified for numerous Classic events, he has also won major walleye tournaments in the North. With fifty-two awards at the last count, Al's long work with teaching youth to fish reached a high point when the U.S. Fish and Wildlife Service used his In-FisherKIDS Camp Fish formula as a nationwide teaching tool. Of all his titles, he prefers that of "Angling Educator," a work he tirelessly pursues.

Ron was inducted into the National Freshwater Fishing Hall of Fame for his contribution and dedication to the sport of freshwater angling and its conservation and history. In pursuing his dream, he has worn many hats— professional guide, tackle and equipment designer, inventor (three patents and thirty unique designs to his credit), tackle manufacturer, professional tournament angler, promoter, writer, publisher, television producer, and radio host. His work in angling theory includes the co-authorship of ten books, the writing of hundreds of published articles, and the production of thousands of radio and TV scripts.

Throughout their professional lives the Lindner brothers blended their work with raising families and growing in their evangelical faith. Ron and wife, Dolores, have seven children (four boys and three girls). Al and his wife, Mary, have two boys. At some point in time every member of both families has worked in one phase or another in the sport fishing industry.

Ron and Al believe that involving the family turns a job, a career, or work into a shared lifestyle.

Most importantly, though, when it's *first light on the water*, Al and Ron Lindner remain incessantly curious fishermen and consummate innovators. So after all these years, for them, there's still nothing that beats a good day's fishing!

I CAN'T REMEMBER A TIME WHEN I DIDN'T
FISH. My earliest recollections are the summers I
spent with my grandmother on a lake near
Hayward, Wisconsin. For me it meant countless
hours of fishing from shore or wading, and occa-
sionally fishing with my uncles in a boat. I also
fished with my older brother, Ron, who was ten
years my senior. If I dug the worms, seined the
minnows, fixed the tackle, and loaded the boat, he
would take me out with him. He told me everyone
starts out first as a "worm boy" apprentice, and for
years I believed him.

When I was sixteen and enjoying one of my many
summers at Grandma's, I entered a Musky Derby
and *won!* I actually got paid for fishing. I was also
interviewed by the local paper and did a snippet
for the TV sports news in nearby Duluth. With that
incredible experience, it was as though my fate was
sealed. I was destined to become a professional
sport fisherman.

Preface

by AL LINDNER

*… it is to be believed,
that all the other Apostles,
after they betook themselves
to follow Christ, betook
themselves to be fishermen
too; for it is certain that the
greater number of them
were found together fishing
by Jesus after His Resur-
rection, as it is recorded in
the twenty-first chapter of
St. John's Gospel, vv. 3,4.*

IZAAK WALTON
The Compleat Angler circa 1653

Growing up in Chicago, I was a mediocre student. If there was a book report to write or a speech to be given, my subject was fishing—always! I had no other hobbies or interests. I didn't hunt, golf, or collect stamps. In my high school yearbook, I stated that my life goal was "to catch a record fish." Even when it came to work, outside of a few odd jobs, fishing or activities directly related to sport fishing are the only work I've ever known.

Even when an army stint took me to Vietnam, where some guys carried the New Testament with them in the field, I carried Buck Perry's *A Spoon Plugging Lesson* or Bill Binkelman's *Night Crawler Secrets*. These tattered, marked, and underlined booklets were as well annotated as many of my fellow soldiers' Bibles. I could even quote many of the passages verbatim. Except for one horrible night in Vietnam, when I didn't know if I would see the light of day, I gave little thought to God or any lesser subjects that required introspection and study.

When I returned home from Vietnam, my piscatorial interests were running high. In 1967 Ron and I moved from Chicago to Minnesota to pursue our dream of setting up a guide service and restarting our tackle-making business. From that point in my life until I retired from fishing the Bassmaster Professional Tournament circuit in 1979, I sometimes clocked as many as three hundred days on the water in a single year. During these halcyon years I also promoted lures, made films for TV, did radio shows, wrote magazine articles with Ron, and did what seemed like an endless parade of sport shows and seminars.

In retrospect, it was an impossible schedule to keep up with for very long. Sooner or later, something had to give. Nevertheless, it was this apprenticeship period that allowed me to explore all types of waters in every part of the country, and I kept discovering new ways to catch more and different types of fish. I learned the art and honed the skills of fishing that would serve me well in the higher ranks of my profession.

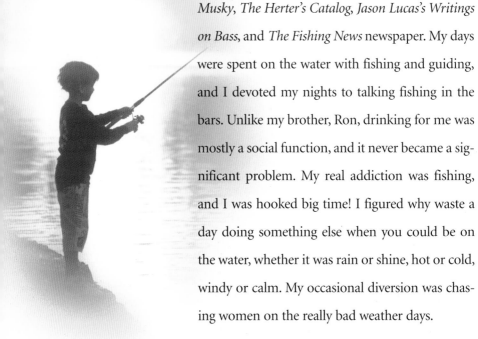

What little time I had for reading during these years was given to books such as *Man Against Musky*, *The Herter's Catalog*, *Jason Lucas's Writings on Bass*, and *The Fishing News* newspaper. My days were spent on the water with fishing and guiding, and I devoted my nights to talking fishing in the bars. Unlike my brother, Ron, drinking for me was mostly a social function, and it never became a significant problem. My real addiction was fishing, and I was hooked big time! I figured why waste a day doing something else when you could be on the water, whether it was rain or shine, hot or cold, windy or calm. My occasional diversion was chasing women on the really bad weather days.

All this time, the God whom I didn't know or care about not only allowed me to have these experiences but preserved me as well. God had a plan for my life that would take my all-consuming passion and turn it into a lifestyle that was both acceptable and ultimately useful to Him. Not surprisingly, a

Some go to church and think about fishing; others go fishing and think about God.

TONY BLAKE

few changes were in order . . . changes that dramatically impacted my "fish all the time" obsession.

The changes seemed to happen fast, all in the span of a few years. First, I got married. Then I got deeply involved with Ron as an owner in the magazine publishing and TV fishing show business. Soon our family grew to four, and then, most importantly, I came to faith in Jesus Christ and was born again. That changed everything.

To tell you the truth, I was relieved after receiving Jesus as Lord of my life that He did not ask me to go into some other endeavor. Here I was in my late thirties, and fishing was the only thing I knew how to do. He graciously allowed me to continue to fish hard in the coming decades, but He made certain that the intensity of my earlier years gave way to a more balanced mode of living. It involved giving up the Bassmaster and BCA Professional Tournament Fishing circuits, something I dearly loved to do, and learning to be content with a few select events every year just to keep my hand in.

During this phase of life, I started attending church regularly, and with my eyes newly opened, I devoured the Bible as I once did books on fishing. I was thrilled to learn that many of Jesus' first inductees (the apostles) were fishermen and that life in the boat was a common theme. It quickly became evident that fishing, much like farming, football, flying, or any other human endeavor, is teeming with life lessons. These lessons, when viewed through God's prism, become very effective modern-day parables.

As I started to share my Christian faith with others, most of whom were fellow fishermen, I found myself naturally using fishing experiences to illustrate and explain the workings of the Kingdom of God. I sensed that God, the ever Supreme Conservationist, would not waste all of my earlier efforts and experiences. Instead, God took the "Gift Within" that He had given me for fishing, and He used the fishing-related experiences both Ron and I had through our long, long years as professional anglers to His own purposes.

I've heard Ron, when speaking to other fishermen about how Jesus Christ saved him from a life of alcoholism, talk about "being scooped up by the gentle net of God's grace" and how "God does not practice catch and release. Instead, He puts us in His live well of eternal life—forever!" While the patterns of our lives as well as our personalities are quite different, both Ron and I have found ourselves constantly sharing our faith through fishing analogies.

In *First Light on the Water*, we retell some of the real-life events and experiences that God has used to illuminate our lives with an understanding that He is alive, concerned, and at work today. He has shown Himself to Ron and me in the most routine events we experience in our lives as well as in the moments of trauma, danger, or during high-charged adventures. God has shown us that we never need to walk in the darkness where we have been, but in the sweet, clear light of life in Jesus Christ.

THROUGHOUT A LIFETIME SPENT ON OCEANS, SEAS, LAKES, RIVERS, AND RESERVOIRS, I'VE HAD COUNTLESS OCCASIONS TO RIDE OUT BIG WAVES AND STRONG WINDS, AND I'VE BEEN SPOOKED BY NEAR LIGHTNING STRIKES. But I've never been truly frightened and have had relatively few harrowing ordeals . . . such as this one.

I was fishing a bass tournament on Lake Minnetonka, a 16,000 acre lake in Minnesota that's broken up into numerous small interconnecting bays. During the pre-fishing phase, I was working alone as the sweltering heat and humidity of early summer worsened into the afternoon. There were thunderstorm warnings out, but it didn't take a weatherman to predict that. The air was downright oppressive. The gray gulls and geese that abound on this waterway had already vanished.

All of a sudden the fish, as they often do in weather like this, "turned on." A cold front pushing through

Chapter One
When God Opens the Door... Go Through It

by RON LINDNER

There is a way that seems right to a man, but in the end it leads to death.

PROVERBS 14:12

seems to instinctively trigger the bass to feed. By now, a huge black cloud rolled up like a wall on the western horizon, and I could hear a constant rumble of thunder in the distance. Knowing I had a fast boat and was close to the landing, I hoped to find one more concentration of bass along the weed line before I made a run for it.

Suddenly the black clouds, some dipping ominously, were coming straight at me. Lightning ignited the sky and thunder boomed everywhere. An eerie yellow-green light descended upon the landscape. With a blast of cold air, the wind picked up. It was time to bail and boogie.

To my consternation, as I turned the key on my 150-horse motor, it sputtered a number of times before turning over. Idling out through the narrows, I spied a large canopied boat dock with long wooden pilings that was sheltered by a big hill. A large cabin cruiser was moored there with an open slip next to it—a perfect refuge from the strong winds.

I hesitated momentarily at this open invitation, but... *at 60 miles per hour*, I thought, *I can make it back to the landing, walk to the nearby restaurant, have a chilled ice tea, and make a couple phone calls.* Without delay, I jacked up the motor, slammed down the throttle, and blasted off, disregarding the speed limit.

As I careened around a point, I realized how badly I had miscalculated the speed of the storm. A black wall of angry-looking, low-hanging clouds, rain, wind, and huge waves slammed into me. At the speed I was going when I hit the first wave, my boat went airborne. Simultaneously, a blast of refrigerated wind caught me in midair and threw my nineteen-foot bass boat on its side. Landing with a bone-jarring bang, I almost flew out, barely able to hang on to the steering wheel.

In the process, I speared a large wave with the nose of the boat. That deluge, as it swept over the front deck, tore loose the front-mounted depth finder and the safety strap on the troll motor. A piece of debris, perhaps the depth finder, hit me along the side of my face and knocked off my prescription sunglasses.

Somehow the boat righted itself, and the engine kept running. I grabbed for my life jacket but realized it was buried in the lockers under boxes of lures, rods, and other fishing gear. Without my glasses and with cold sheets of water and mothball-size hail beating down on me, I fumbled to hit the bilge pump switch on the dashboard—click . . . click . . . click—nothing!

The cockpit was now shin deep with rising water. I knew I had to get the boat moving and "on plane," and I did. Advancing toward the landing dock, I saw a flotilla of craft crowded everywhere. They too were caught short by the storm, making it impossible to dock there. Then the boat suddenly started a foreboding list.

Relentless sheets of rain continued to obscure my vision, and I knew my last shot for shelter was a canal nearby with a bridge. If I could get under the bridge and out of the rain, I might be able to get the bilge pump running. But as I got closer to the bridge, I saw a number of boats piled side to side, and my boat was listing dangerously. My only alternative was to beach the boat, but both sides of the canal's entrance were piled four-feet deep with huge rocks.

I pushed the throttle, but the list was so bad I could no longer power the boat. I knew it was going down. As the craft dipped, I scampered up the side like sailors on a torpedoed ship, and as I jumped off and swam toward shore, the old "this can't be happening to me" refrain went through my mind. Then the boat "turtled," totally flipping upside down.

As I stood in waist-deep water, soaked to the bone and shivering cold, I was proof of the old mariner saying that was fashioned after the apostle Paul's storm saga in Acts 27: "the sea is unforgiving of stupidity." Once I pulled away from that protected dock, I pushed myself out from under God's protective umbrella and paid the price. Eventually, my boat was recovered at great cost, and it never ran well again. I hope I learned my lesson.

REFLECTION

by AL LINDNER

When God opens a door in your life, don't ever pass it by. I know with absolute surety that God saved Ron a spot at the dock that day, but Ron thought he had a better way—his way. Doors open, and doors close . . . sometimes forever. The laws of God's kingdom are every bit as certain in their operation as the laws of the wind and rain, and if we stubbornly refuse what He provides in His grace and love, we will reap the consequences. The decision of a moment can determine one's whole future. A time comes to every person when he must obey or refuse God's provision—and know it in his heart. May we be quick to go through the doors He opens and never miss precious gifts He has for each of us.

Chapter Two

Guidance and
Answered
Prayer

by AL LINDNER

The steps of a good
man are ordered
by the LORD.

PSALM 37:23 KJV

FACING UNCERTAINTY IN ANY ENDEAVOR OF LIFE CAN BE DAUNTING. Whether it's leaving home for the first time or launching into business for yourself, once you step out into the big unknown the alarm bells can ring loud and often. Some folks say they enjoy the challenge, but most of us find it a bit unnerving.

Every spring season for fifteen years Ron and I had aired a series of one-hour TV fishing specials on a host of Midwestern broadcast channels. We styled the format around what we were comfortable with, and it worked very successfully. But in 1984 satellite and cable TV began transforming our industry. We knew viewing patterns, syndication methodology, and cost of airtime were all in a state of flux. If we failed to make a move, our show would wither and die on the vine.

Our first step was to take our situation to God. Praying with Ron and Mike Simpson, a Christian brother who worked with us in television, we dedicated the new program to God and asked for His grace and guidance and a blessing on our labors. Then we began contacting every satellite and cable outlet that was either online or coming online and that might offer our type of show. Based upon the good reputation and the prominence we had gained as well as the awards we had garnered for our program, we thought we would be welcomed with open arms.

We may say of angling as Dr. Boteler said of strawberries:

"Doubtless God could have made a better berry,

but doubtless God never did;"

and so, if I may be judge, God never did make a more

calm, quiet, innocent recreation than angling.

SIR IZAAK WALTON, *The Compleat Angler*

I flew to ESPN in New York full of confidence but found we couldn't even get a hearing in the Big Apple. Mike went to CBN, where he had some contacts, but they weren't interested either. Ron made his pitch to the TBS, WGN, USA, and Discovery networks. All of it netted *absolutely nothing!*

It was baffling . . . as though every door had slammed shut. Little by little our confidence turned to anxiety as a touch of fear and doubt reared its ugly head.

We kept searching and found that TNN, the Nashville Network, was beginning to gain cable outlets and satellite viewership. Its demographic focus was right for us—downhome people who would be interested in fishing. We also met several Christians in key positions at TNN and their satellite business, the Grand Ole Opry, who made us feel very comfortable. But TNN's audience reach at that time, when compared to ESPN, USA, CBN, or TBS, was minuscule. With our options running out, we resigned ourselves to the situation and cut a deal.

Still, plenty of questions loomed in our minds. We had prayed hard for guidance and God's blessing, but the stations that reached the bigger audiences, which we felt we needed to make the show a success, gave us the cold shoulder. And all we ended up with was a small country music focus cable outlet. Though we were very disappointed, we decided to give our best and hope for something better. I don't recall that we even thanked God at the time for opening the door at TNN.

Fast forward a decade.

TNN experienced astonishing growth and so did we. In fact, during one particular year, in the accumulative four quarters, *In-Fisherman Television* was seen by more viewers than any other television fishing show on planet earth.

And on top of that, during these phenomenal growth years, *In-Fisherman* media network of magazines, radio, books, videos, and tournament circuit was established as a nationwide entity.

Do we serve an awesome God who answers prayers . . . or what?

REFLECTION

by RON LINDNER

In retrospect, God could not have answered our prayers better than putting us on TNN when He did. As the world of satellite and cable networks shook out, it was the absolute best outlet for our show at that time. God knows well in advance what is best for His children. The older I get, the more I realize that what might look in the short term to be a stingy or even a no answer to prayer is always, in the final analysis, the right thing . . . in the right place . . . at the right time. ⊰

Chapter Three

Don't Look for Answers in the Devil's Gap

by RON LINDNER

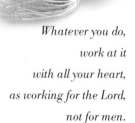

Whatever you do,
work at it
with all your heart,
as working for the Lord,
not for men.

COLOSSIANS 3:23

WITH ITS ALMOST ONE MILLION SPRAWL-ING ACRES AND 14,000 ISLANDS, LAKE OF THE WOODS ON THE MINNESOTA/ONTARIO BORDER SPORTS SOME INTRIGUING NAMES FOR ITS AREAS—Dead Man's Portage, The Corkscrew, The Bowling Alley, The Tangle, and Fall Dangerous. Then there are two even more ominous sounding places, The Devil's Gap and Hades, that are forever etched in my memory.

In the early 1990s, the opportunity finally came to get my oldest son Bill to fish a bass tournament with me. Though a renowned wildlife, fish, and food photographer, and one of the best all-around multispecies anglers I know, Bill was no fan of competitive fishing. For years I badgered him to be my tournament partner, but he would shrug his shoulders and say, "I'm too high strung for this kind of thing."

But after many years of working for a major book publishing firm, Bill decided to strike out on his own as a free-lance photographer, and he needed a fair chunk of money to purchase some specialized photography equipment. I told him that if he'd be my fishing partner for the Kenora Bass International (KBI), he could keep the entire purse if we won. In this 227 boat field, first place was $50,000 (Canadian), and even second- and third-place finishes paid fairly well. To my pleasant surprise, Bill agreed.

For many years my relationship with Bill had been strained. However, by this time I had grown in my faith and was maturing in my walk with God, and Bill had recently made a recommitment to the Lord. I hoped that if we worked together toward a common goal for over a week as equal boat "partners," we might interact as friends rather than the strictly father/son relationship we had.

"All you need to be a fisherman
is patience and a worm."
HERB SHRINER

I also thought I might be able to use the tournament to impart some wisdom on how to run his new business. The way we plan and prepare and execute the strategy to fish a tournament relates directly to business. For example, poorly maintained equipment or time management can beat you in a fishing tournament as easily as in a photography shoot. There was also a spiritual component that I hoped Bill would always do in his business—we would also ask God for help and guidance in the task at hand. And we would pray together for safety as I always do—not only for us but for all the competitors.

I should note that in a tournament or any other competitive sport, it is my personal belief that unless God has a sovereign reason to do otherwise, He usually lets normal events unravel, and the "best" prepared person will usually win the event. I also believe that you must do the preparation—do your homework and pre-fish. It is foolish and presumptuous to say a fast prayer and expect God to bless you with a win when you are unprepared.

There were a number of heavy hitters—"tournament legends"—fishing this event, including my son James and brother Al. After a long hiatus from competitive fishing, I felt a personal pressure to prove to myself that "I still had it," and a strong finish would go a long way in reigniting the competitive spark. Bill too had something to prove. Being in his first tournament, he wanted to know if he could "run with the big dogs."

So together we set about pre-fishing in dead earnest. Over and over we said to each other, "We came here to win!" Bill had the necessary raw fishing talent, and through long experience I knew tournament fishing tactics and strategies that lead to wins.

As we pre-fished, a pattern slowly began to emerge. We found that big smallmouth would hang along the chains of buoys that mark the many rock shoals of the lake. We were not targeting the shoals as much as the chains and buoys adjacent to them. When we would run and gun the thirty-two buoy milk route, we would get only about nine bites . . . not a lot of fish, but they were all big. If we could boat six fish of this size on both days of the tournament, we knew we could win. We had also found a number of smaller fish concentrated in a place called Hades as well as an area called the Devil's Gap.

After four days of practice, we were definitely "on fish, and big fish." Our game plan was set, and all we had to do was implement it "by the numbers." I had never felt more confident in a tournament before or since, and we might have even been a little cocky.

At daybreak the smell of oil and gas from the engine exhausts mixed with the adrenaline in our veins during the takeoff, which only heightened the excitement. We had six identical rods and reels spooled with six-pound test Trilene strapped on the deck. All were identically rigged in the same size, color, and type of lure—a $\frac{3}{32}$ ounce black mushroom jig head with a 3" black Berkley Power Grub. That's how confident we were of our pattern.

The first day went just about as planned. We first went for smaller fish to fill out our limit, then culled them out with the less numerous but bigger fish on the marker buoys. By day's end, we were in third place and just ten ounces off first place! We were psyched for the next day.

The second and final day, however, we opted not to go for the smaller fish. We needed six big fish to make up for our weight deficit, so why waste time? We started working the buoy chain pattern right off the bat, but an overnight cold front had blown through, switching the wind to the northwest. It was blowing hard and right down the alleys of markers we were fishing. The water temperature had dropped, and the bass were really slow.

It took us an hour and a half to boat our first fish, but it was a lunker! An hour and a half later and countless markers behind us, we caught a second big fish. By noon we had only three of the six fish we needed. Then another long lull set in as the wind increased and the white caps tossed us about, making the boat hard to handle.

By one o'clock and stuck at three fish, the alarm bells of doubt started to clang. With a 3:00 P.M. flight weigh-in, we only had until 2:30 to leave this area in order to not get disqualified. In my heart, I was asking God why the stinking wind . . . of all times now . . . and why not wind from the other direction, and why right down the "chute" where we needed to fish. Hadn't we worked hard? Hadn't we worked smart?

At 1:15 I said to Bill, "Let's go to Hades or Devil's Gap and try for our limit with a few smaller fish. A smaller check is better than nothing."

From a purely professional tournament angler's viewpoint, this was good strategy. But Bill looked straight at me and said, "We came here to win."

About then I started getting feedback from the Lord deep in my heart. "Didn't I hear you tell James and Al that you two had the best pattern on the lake? And didn't I see in your magazines, books, and TV series that you purport to know how to fish well? So why don't you stay with it, quit your whining, and fish." That sobered me for a while.

Minutes later we caught the fourth fish—it was a biggie. But by 2:15 we didn't have another hit, so I mentioned Hades or Devil's Gap again.

Bill shook his head and said, "Let's just stay with it."

Five minutes later Bill caught our fifth fish . . . another good-sized one, pushing my roller coaster confidence on the upswing again. With fifteen minutes left and thinking out loud, I said to Bill, "God's guidance had us stay with it. We'll get that last fish soon."

But as I watched the last minutes tick down, I knew that if there was heavy boat congestion in the channel, we might not even make it in time. I finally told Bill, "We gotta go!"

I am constantly amazed by the many ways God meets with us

and how often He communicates

through what is familiar to us personally.

In our lives, God has often used lures, rods, and boats

to bring fishing-related lessons we can easily identify with.

Listen closely, and you'll hear Him speaking to you as well.

You don't have to go somewhere special to hear Him.

Because He loves you, He speaks in words you will understand.

AL LINDNER

We bailed with one fish short of the limit, and I felt totally dejected. I had missed God's guidance and had instead listened to the echoes of my own emotions. We should have gone to Hades for small bass so we could at least net a decent check and save face with a limit.

Flying down the lake at top speed, we made it to the weigh-in area with five minutes to spare. In the distance I could see the continuous line of boats racing toward the finish line. Then glancing to my left, I saw a rock sticking out of the water along the shoreline where I'd had a strike but missed the fish during the practice days.

Acting on an impulse, I maneuvered toward the rock and cut the engine. Bobbing in the water without power and struggling to get my balance, I grabbed the first rod I could get free, flipped the jig out to the rock, and immediately felt weight on the end. Thinking I was hung up, I yanked not once but twice, hoping to free the lure. Then all of a sudden a big smallie leapt four feet high out of the water!

Both Bill and I were stunned. Bill stumbled to his feet and fumbled to get the net loose from the tie-down. With the trolling motor still strapped down and the wind blowing, we were bouncing all over in the waves. Fighting the fish, up and back and under the boat, I somehow got the fish near enough for Bill to lean over and, with one lightning stab, scoop up the fish.

Knowing we had but seconds left, I dropped the rod and put the fish with line and lure still in his mouth into the live well and raced to the finish line . . . making it in with thirty seconds to spare.

Coming off plane, I looked at Bill, who was grinning from ear to ear, and confidently said, "We just won the tournament."

And we did . . . by three ounces! Suddenly all those small fish in Hades and the Devil's Gap looked very small.

REFLECTION

by RON LINDNER

Later in prayer and meditation, the Lord spoke to my heart and said, "Would the win have been any sweeter if you had caught all the fish in the first hour? Would you have learned anything? When things don't go as smooth or as fast as you think they should, your faith wavers and you grasp for easy solutions...usually your own solutions and usually in the wrong places. Jonah and Abraham did the same. Instead of staying with what you know is right, you bail for quick fixes like the Devil's Gap or Hades and settle for much less than what could have been." Despite that, God used it to bring Bill and me together, and over the years we've grown very close. Between the KBI and the allied Canadian Rainy Lake Tournament, we've racked up many top-ten finishes together and had a lot of fun doing it. ⤢

OF ALL THE THINGS WE HAVE PRINTED AND RUN ON TELEVISION OVER THE YEARS, the one that prompted the most heart-searching questions, comments, and opinions was our fish symbol. For us it has a long and hallowed history.

In the early fall of 1983, I returned to my office after a day on the water to check my mail and was surprised to find an insertion order for a beer ad to be placed in our fishing magazine. When we had pursued this type of advertising previously, we were told our publication was too small. But now the opportunity we had waited for was right in my hands. The ad was tastefully done, extolling the beauty of the outdoors, and only had a small bottle and logo at the bottom.

Our magazine was eight years old at the time, and circulation was up to 100,000. We had been on the newsstands for a few years, primarily around the Upper Midwest. Every small publisher at that time coveted alcohol or tobacco ads. Besides paying top

Chapter

Four

The Fish Symbol

by AL LINDNER

Whosoever therefore shall confess me before men, him will I confess also before my Father which is in heaven.

MATTHEW 10:32 KJV

dollar, these ads signaled to other ad agencies that your publication had arrived, and often new ads for similar competitive products would follow. Usually these companies would run a series of consecutive ads that were for us, "found money"—money outside the endemic boat, motor, rod, reel, and lure advertisers we regularly serviced. These ads might also be door openers for commercials for our TV and radio shows. This was a very big deal!

To put my reaction to the ad into perspective, I need to give a bit of family background. By this time Ron and his wife, Dolores, and my wife, Mary, had been believers for a few years, but I had just accepted Jesus as my Savior only six months earlier. I was in the "immersed in the Bible" stage, and each day was a new revelation for me.

Back then the Christian fish symbol was not nearly in the widespread use it gets today. You might have seen a sticker on an occasional car, but that was about it. A year earlier Dolores had read Deuteronomy 6:9, "Write them on the doorframes of your houses and on your gates," so she put the fish symbol on their mailbox at home. Seeing it, Ron decided to put one on his boat as well. That was it, and no one thought much more about it.

But over the past year, Ron had dabbled with it more and more, adding a cross to the fish. And he had been trying some variations of using it in conjunction with our logo. A few months before the ad came, Ron, Dolores, Mary, and I had met and agreed that we would put the words "Jesus Is Lord" over the entry of our building. With this sign up, we had held hands and prayed, dedicating our company to God. With that dedication, we also decided to add the fish symbol to our corporate logo, which was going to involve a vast amount of printing plates, artwork, and preprinted material as well as patches, jackets, hats, etc.

So, with all this going on, I looked at the beer ad and felt what some Christians call a "check in my spirit." Others would call it a strong gut feeling to wait a moment because something isn't right.

Make no mistake about it. These were struggling years we were facing. We needed the money "now," and this ad could open the gates to a lot more "of kind" revenue. This infusion of capital could very well take us to the next level. And the ad was in no way offensive. We had run boat ads with bikini-clad models that were much less tasteful. So I'm thinking to myself, *What's your problem with this ad? Are you turning into a prude or something?* Still, I wasn't at peace with going ahead with the ad.

So I called our first family business meeting. Before this, either Ron or I decided something, and that was it. I showed them the ad, and our wives immediately gave it the "thumbs down." They, however, didn't have to go out and peddle ads. Then Ron said he was leaning in their direction. I confess I was torn. Ron finally said that since I was in charge of advertising, I should make the final call.

That night I prayed and pondered it. How do you draw the line on ads? Should you even try? Is there a difference between bad taste and bad morals? What about smokeless chew tobacco and cheeky bikini boat ads? How about ads for real estate hustlers?

There was something else involved here. The fish symbol was going on all our materials, including our media kits, and it was possible that some of our key sales outlets were getting offended. If we now started getting self-righteous about ads, what then? We couldn't afford to lose an occasional subscriber who might be offended, let alone risk having the big ad agencies and firms we derived our primary income from regard us as religious kooks.

Oh, give me grace to catch a fish
So big that even I
When talking of it afterwards
May have no need to lie.
ANONYMOUS

Those questions bombarded my mind. Would we ever grow beyond a narrow niche fishing magazine and regional TV fishing show if we painted ourselves into such a tight corner?

That night I read Proverbs 16:3: "Commit to the LORD whatever you do, and your plans will succeed." It was clear to me that we had done the committing when we first displayed the fish symbol, and now it was equally clear that it was time to put our money where our mouth was. I knew I had my answer, and a peace followed.

The next morning I told Ron of my decision, and we made it our policy to not take any alcohol or tobacco ads—with no exceptions. If anything else that was questionable came up, we would consider them on a case-by-case basis.

Over the ensuing months we received more ads from different accounts than we ever had before. Lots more! We even got ads from firms we had a hard time cracking before. And all were nice and tasteful.

There is no question in my mind that this was a confirmation from God that we were on the right track. And despite criticism and difficulties, we've never had a moment's regret. The public display of the fish symbol reminds us that we are to depend upon God as our source and not look to any place or anyone else.

REFLECTION

by DOLORES LINDNER

When we sold our business to a New York publishing conglomerate, things naturally changed. The fish came off the logo, and "Jesus Is Lord" came off the doorway. And well they should, because these were our personal statements. Still, I cannot help but remember how blessed I was the first time we used "the fish" as our television sign-off. And every time the show closed, this symbol reminded me that God was truly our provider.

Over the years our company has been honored and blessed with many awards, trophies, and mementos, but when we left the company, the "Jesus Is Lord" sign and the fish symbol etched in glass on an entry window were the first things we took with us. Jesus was right: where your treasure is, there your heart is also. ⤨

Chapter Five

Thoroughly Equipped

by RON LINDNER

All Scripture is God-breathed and is useful for teaching, rebuking, correcting and training in righteousness, so that the man of God may be thoroughly equipped for every good work.

2 TIMOTHY 3:16-17

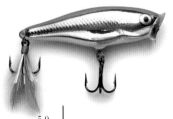

WHEN IT COMES TO SPORTS FISHING, I LIVE BY THE OLD BOY SCOUT RULE, "BE PREPARED." For me that includes a complete array of lures and paraphernalia packed in complete order in the boat with solutions for all fishing eventualities and possibilities. That's my rule.

At an annual charity fundraising bass tournament held by former Minnesota Viking coach Dennis Green, I discovered a new life lesson about being "thoroughly prepared." It was a team event, and I was paired with a good friend, who is both a professional tournament angler and a believer. The tournament was early in the season, so we determined to check the shallows for pre-spawn and spawning largemouth during the pre-fishing.

On the first practice day we found a wind-protected bay that had warmed early and had the right bottom content to attract staging fish. We skirted the shoreline and scanned the water not only for fish but also for the telltale signs of use, such as swept

50

nests and log brushings. It wasn't long before we came upon a dead give-away—yellowish plate-size depressions all over the shallows. We didn't make a cast, but merely noted the spots and kept on looking.

Leaving this area, we also fished a number of other locations and patterns—specifically, staging bass on two large main lake weedy flats. Careful not to "burn" these spots, we caught just enough fish on spinner baits to indicate the numbers of bass present. By the end of the second day of pre-fishing, we had our game plan in place. If we drew an early flight, we would fish the smaller protected bay. But if we drew a later flight, we would head for the large main flats, figuring the small bay would be jammed with boats.

Well, we drew number 90, which put us at the back of the pack. Going directly to the flats, we caught fish and limited out by noon, but with mostly "buck bass" (around 2 pounds). To win the tournament was going to require fish over 3 pounds, and we were confounded at not being able to move up. So we ran here, ran there, trying to upgrade our catch, using the same spinner baits. Late in the afternoon when we were on the way back to the weigh-in site, we stopped in the small spawning bay. No one was there, but that wasn't strange. We were in the last flight, and most of the other boats had already headed back. Nonetheless, we decided to put the troll motor down and make a quick pass with the spinner baits.

"Even a bad day of fishing
is better than a good day of work."

UNKNOWN

All of a sudden, bang, bang, bang, we caught three fish. Not monsters, but large enough to cull three of our fish up, and they were the largest we caught all day. With time running out, we left and went back to the weigh-in site. After weighing in, we went to the scoreboard, which was flanked by all the contestants. A big bag of fish, averaging almost $3\frac{3}{4}$ pounds per fish, was leading, and the team that brought it in eventually won the tournament.

After the event, we got together with the other players in a time-honored post-tournament tradition and indulged ourselves in the could-of's, would-of's, and should-of's of the tournament. Not only had the small spawning bay put up the winning fish, but the first-place team caught them "dead sticking" Sluggos—a soft plastic minnow-shaped bait. Besides this, the fish in the bay did not turn on until afternoon, after most of the early boats had left. The winners pretty much had the bay and fish all to themselves. The winners had left shortly before we arrived and had upgraded right till the end. The presentation was a slow, almost motion-less retrieve. The big fish simply did not want anything fast moving.

My tournament partner and I eyed each other, and the recriminations started. How could such an obvious solution escape us? Especially since we both love dead sticking and pride ourselves in being good at it. With my boat locker filled with a veritable arsenal of lures, why didn't we even try "soft plastics"? Although we knew about the solution, had the equipment and experience to use it well, we failed to employ it. We concluded that we simply fell into a rut with the spinner baits.

On the three-hour drive back home after the tournament, I mulled things over in my head and chided myself for missing the "dead stick" pattern. It struck me how similar this was to other situations in my life where I have failed to use all the spiritual equipment God has given me. As a result, I missed God's best or suffered needlessly.

One such recent incident involved a lawsuit that regarded a very complex trademark and copyright issue, with complications that ran back almost twenty years. As a general rule the Scripture warns us to stay out of man's courts if at all possible, and over the years we heeded that counsel. The Scripture also plainly tells us that brothers in the Lord should never go to court with each other (1 CORINTHIANS 6:6). But this was a wrangle over which of our corporations owned a specific copyright. So we were called into court and had to defend ourselves.

Catch and release fishing is a lot like golf.
You don't have to eat the ball
to have a good time.

UNKNOWN

My first mistake was that right from the start I took the suit personally… very personally, and that led to errors in judgment. Although I prayed about it in a general way, I let some bad feelings enter the picture and breed an atmosphere of ongoing confrontation. I felt unjustly attacked, and that we were being played for a patsy. If they thought we were just going to stand there and take a slap in the face like this, they had another thing coming. If they wanted to fight, then fight it is . . . and it went on for over four horrible, agonizing years. As litigation unfolded and several law firms, insurance companies, and different judicial jurisdictions became involved, it absorbed all my time and energy, as only litigation of this kind can, and took on a life of its own. I was caught hook, line, and sinker, and I'm sure the devil played me like a 1-pound crappie on a musky rod.

The second mistake was that although I knew this battle involved spiritual warfare, I did not fully put on the whole armor of God (EPHESIANS. 6:10-18). I did not pray with *all* types of prayer or with persistent supplication. There were many, many things I could have done spiritually that I didn't. And the longer this ordeal went on, the more of a flesh fight it became for me. Were our attorneys making progress? Were they doing enough and would they counter the opposers' legal tricks? Was the judge going to give us a summary judgment? Why couldn't people see the facts?

I became dependent upon all those things that you can't really trust. It wasn't until everyone involved, and especially me, started to get fed up with the whole mess that I started to truly pray for the opposition (and for me this wasn't easy). I wasn't praying that the opposition would see the errors of their ways and we could come to some equitable compromise. I started praying for their well-being and for their families. This was the closest I could get to expressing the *agape* love that the Scripture plainly tells us "never fails" (1 CORINTHIANS 13:8).

Soon after my "true prayers" started, we got the news that the primary suit had been settled in our favor. By now there were suits and counter suits. Then we heard that the other suit also looked favorable for us. At this point I made a phone call to the executive of the other company. This was our first contact since the suit started, and both of us had been advised by the attorneys to not do this. Nonetheless, I asked for a lunch with him alone, and he accepted. Forty-five minutes later we shook hands and left the problem behind us, except for the mounds of paperwork to close it out legally. *It was finally over!*

That lawsuit wasted an enormous amount of time, money, energy, and talent that could have been directed to positive endeavors. But as things unfolded, I fell into a rut as I did with the spinner baits. I failed to use all the spiritual equipment that God had given me and instead relied on flesh and blood tactics. Knowing the words, "not by might nor by power, but by my Spirit, says the LORD Almighty" (ZECH. 4:6), is not the same as living them.

After a recent disaster I heard a man say, "Things got so bad I had to totally rely on God." Why is that? Speaking from experience, don't ever wait to reach out for something transcendent. Take the concerns of your heart immediately to God and leave them with Him.

REFLECTION

by AL LINDNER

I am constantly amazed by the many ways God meets with us and how often He communicates through what is familiar to us personally. In Ron's life, God has often used lures, rods, and boats to bring fishing-related lessons he can easily identify with. David, a young shepherd, understood God's goodness in terms of green pastures and still waters. Peter, an experienced fisherman, knew that God supplies all our needs and can even put a coin in a fish's mouth to help him out. Recently, I read the book A Personal Journey *by astrophysicist Hugh Ross in which he tells how he came to understand the workings of God through "heat-releasing radioisotopes," "mesopheric ozone," "supernovae emissions," and "high energy particles."*

Listen closely, and you'll hear Him speaking to you as well. You don't have to go somewhere special to hear Him. Because He loves you, He speaks in words you will understand. ✢

I REMEMBER THE MOMENT I RECEIVED THE PHONE CALL FROM MY WIFE, MARY. It was a Friday night in July 1997, and I was alone in my motel room. I had been fishing the Canadian Bass Championship on Rainy Lake.

"Al," she spoke slowly, "the mammogram I took on Wednesday showed a lump on my breast. The doctor has scheduled me for surgery on Tuesday at 7 A.M."

It took a while for her words to sink in, but when they finally did I felt their force and was glad I was sitting down. My first response was "Mary, let's pray," which we did. And then I said, "I'm packing up and coming home right away."

Mary's response was as calm as the evening lake. "No," she said. "Stay and fish the tournament. There's really nothing you can do here, and I'll be just fine."

Chapter Six

Expect a Good Report

by AL LINDNER

The thief cometh not, but for to steal, and to kill, and to destroy: I am come that they might have life, and that they might have it more abundantly.

JOHN 10:10 KJV

63

We talked for a while and prayed again before saying good-bye. Then I took a long walk . . . with God. We needed to talk, and I had a lot on my heart. By the time I was nearly back to my room, I felt a peace begin to come over me. And when I was crossing the parking lot of a tire store across the street from the motel, I heard the Lord's still small voice whisper, "Don't worry. Mary will be okay."

With that amazing reassurance, I finished out the tournament through Sunday and immediately headed home. That evening and all day Monday, Mary was amazingly calm. She went about her normal routine, read healing scriptures, listened to tapes, and I heard her quote "by his stripes I am healed and whole" (1 PETER 2:24). That's my Mary for you.

"It's a done deal. I'll be fine," she said, recalling a song we sing in church that declares: "Whose report are you going to believe? I will believe the report of the Lord!" So Mary's response to the doctor was always: "I'm expecting a good report!"

Early Tuesday morning we arrived at the hospital along with one of our church pastors. He and I laid hands on Mary and prayed for her, and then the nurses wheeled her out to the surgery room. Forty-five minutes later the doctor came back out.

"Mary's lump was cancerous," he said. "We cut it out along with twelve lymph nodes, which have been sent to Minneapolis. We should have the report back on Thursday."

I was stunned momentarily. This was not the "good report" I was expecting. But again, the peace of God came over my heart, and I heard the words: "She'll be okay."

As I went into the recovery room, the doctor was telling Mary the lump was cancerous. Again, she looked at me, smiled, and said, "I'll be just fine, Al. I'm expecting a good report."

Mary was checked out of the hospital on Wednesday, and as we drove home she was all smiles—praising God and laughing! She hadn't even taken a pain pill yet. (I would have taken the whole bottle by then.) To her the surgery was nothing more than a trip to the dentist to get a tooth filled. Her words to me were: "Honey, I'm fine."

That night Mary slept on a recliner. She still had a drain tube attached, and the recliner provided the only comfortable sleeping position.

I went to bed alone, unaware of what I was about to face. For the first time, doubt and fear came over me like a heavy blanket. I had the craziest, most insane thoughts I could ever imagine—thoughts only the author of insanity himself, the devil, could send my way. The fiery darts of the master deceiver battered me with dread and mistrust throughout the night as I stood on these words from God: "For God has not given us the spirit of fear, but of power and of love and of a sound mind" (2 TIMOTHY 1:7, NKJV).

"The best time to go fishing
is when you can get away."

ROBERT TRAVER

I rose early the next morning, having survived one of the most miserable nights of my life, and walked downstairs to check on Mary. It was daybreak, and long shafts of golden light were streaming through the window and casting a soft glow about her. She was sleeping like a baby with a smile on her face.

Nevertheless, another wave of fear rushed over me, defying the peace I saw so evidently on Mary's face. I went outside where I could quote scriptures out loud and came boldly before the throne of God. I cried, "Lord, you say in your Word—" when suddenly it felt as though my arm was grabbed and shaken. I heard the Lord speak to my heart: "*Stop! I said she will be okay!*"

With a big sigh of relief, I went back inside, having finally gotten the message from my head to my heart.

We waited four or five days for the report to come back. When the doctor finally called with the good news that everything was fine, Mary looked at me and said, "I knew that. I was expecting a good report." We both praised and thanked God for His Word and the power of prayer.

Mary underwent thirty-two days of radiation and was put on medication for five years. It has been over four years, and she has remained whole and healed—cancer-free.

REFLECTION

by MARY LINDNER

I lost my sister to breast cancer in 1999. The devil returned to try to put thoughts of doubt in Al and me. We stood on the faith-building words of Mark 11:22-24 and Proverbs 3:1-3. I now carry those verses in a locket Al gave me. I believed that what God said was mine...really truly mine. As I prayed to have that mountain of cancer removed from my body, the Lord was faithful to answer my prayer. Get to know His Word and His promises for you, and once you do, never let them go. Always expect a good report!

Chapter Seven

When Things Go South

by AL LINDNER

Not that I am implying that I was in any personal want, for I have learned how to be content (satisfied to the point where I am not disturbed or disquieted) in whatever state I am.

PHILIPPIANS 4:11 AMP

I HAD THE INVITATION IN MY HAND, AND, MAN, IT FELT GOOD. Glancing out my window at the thick blanket of snow and the cold gray light of a Minnesota winter, the thought of fishing for big bass in 70+ degrees in Florida seemed like a dream. I love ice fishing, but I was ready to pitch the winter gear for some fun in the sun.

The letter was from the Bass Pro Shops, inviting me to fish the upcoming Legends tournament in early February 2001. The event was to be held on the Disney Lakes in Orlando, Florida. I'd seen several fishing shows televised on these lakes in the past, and if half the stories I'd heard about the size and number of bass in these lakes were true, this tournament was for me. Although I'd been invited to the tournament in previous years, because of other commitments I'd never been able to make it.

Mary and I decided to drive down early, and I'd do some fishing with Ron. He and Dolores spend their winters in Florida on the St. Lucie River and are only a few hours from Orlando. We fished a few days on the river for snook and tarpon, then spent three days on the Stick Marsh fishing bass with shiners, which I'd never done before. We absolutely slaughtered the bass . . . BIG bass, and I discovered that shiners are the only way to go when you want to catch lots of Floridas early in the season. They say shiners produce at a 5:1 ratio over artificial at that time of year.

The morning I headed for the tournament and the rules meeting, I was as confident and as fired up as I could possibly be. I love the competitive

side of fishing, and I fish tournaments because I believe I can win. I know the importance of confidence in winning, and I always take that into any tournament I fish. Besides, because of my own busyness of putting together our television series, I hadn't fished a tournament for a long time and was looking forward to seeing old friends and competing on the water with them again before a national audience.

The tournament is by invitation only, and the Who's Who of tournament bass fishing were all there—Rick Clunn, Kevin VanDam, Jay Yelas, Mark Davis, David Fritts, Jimmy Houston, and Gary Klein, just to name a few. Then there were the other greats, the "legends," such as Tom Mann, Johnny Morris, Billy Westmoreland, and others who have made a major impact on sport fishing.

We had one day of practice, and I needed to get a good look at the water. Most of the fishermen knew these waters like the back of their hand, but I had never fished this system. I caught about twenty-five bass, with the biggest being around 3½ pounds, and saw an abundance of fish. At the evening banquet, we drew fishing partners as well as got our takeoff numbers, and I was the second boat out. Wow! It didn't get much better than that. I knew . . . knew with certainty . . . where I was going to open and that I'd get a quick limit.

"Man can learn a lot from fishing—

when the fish are biting,

no problem in the world is big enough

to be remembered."

OA BATTISTAA

What followed through the next two days was the absolute worst performance of my entire competitive fishing career . . . and I went into it with supreme confidence. It got so bad, I started to talk to myself. Everything I did didn't work. I could not put a decent fish in the boat to save my life, despite other guys rolling in big fish all around me. For some reason I could not get it together. By the end of the first day, I was out of the running. No chance of even coming close.

But my partner, an amateur, was doing well. On the second day he was in the hunt to win the fully rigged Tracker boat and trailer, which is the first-place prize for the Pros guest angler. Determining to help guide him to score big time (and hoping to save face by at least putting him on the winning bag of fish), I followed a weed line that drops from 10 to 16 feet on a small point. We were both cranking Risto Raps, but then my partner switched to a rod with a white jig-n-craw and made a cast away from the break line I was following. Out of the corner of my eye I saw the bait hit the water and bang! a 4½ pounder hit. This fish added nicely to my partner's weight.

I moved the boat out to where he caught the fish, a 16-foot flat with fish suspended over nothing—no structure, no cover—just chasing bait. It wasn't long before I heard my partner set the hook again, and he was

into a nice fish—*the fish* that will win the boat! I reached for the net just as the fish broke water, and I could see that the crankbait was only lip hooked on the last treble hook. The wind was blowing us away, the bass was shaking its head and coming across the back of the boat, and I could see it's only skin hooked now and about to come off any second. I stretched out as far as I could reach, touched the end of the fish, went to roll it in, and the hook caught the net. The fish shook loose, wobbled on the edge of the net, and fell out. I was crushed. Away swam the fish along with my partner's new Tracker boat and trailer hooked to its tail.

The next morning I packed up the boat and headed for home. The two-and-a-half-day drive from Orlando to Minnesota gave me a lot of time

to think about what had happened. There was only one angler who finished lower than I did in the tournament. As a competitor who loves to win, I was disgusted with my performance and kept asking myself what I could have done different to change it. Well, I never figured that out.

But as I drove across the country, the realization came over me that I was amazingly blessed to live in this great nation of ours. Here I was free to pursue my dreams and make a living doing what I love—fishing! I support myself through a lifestyle, not a job. I had just fished with some of the best fishermen in the world on some great water with beautiful facilities and every convenience. Can anyone who gets to do what I do ever say they had a bad day?

REFLECTION

by MARY LINDNER

Neither Al nor I will ever forget this tournament. It truly changed Al's life. I should know, having listened to him mumbling to himself for hundreds of miles on our drive home from Florida. To watch the peace of God come over him was like the calm and serenity that come over a quiet flowing river as the wind dies down. Contentment does not mean a life free from trouble. But when the peace of God comes to rule in your heart, and when the joy of the Lord becomes your strength, the sense of divine blessing overflows the heart! Then we can say with David, "Why are you downcast, O my soul? Why so disturbed within me? Put your hope in God, for I will yet praise him, my Savior and my God" (PSALM 42:5).

OF ALL THE VARIOUS BUSINESS VENTURES that Al and Mary and Dolores and I put our hands to over the years, perhaps the most special one was also the most frustrating for me personally.

In 1984, after considerable prayer and seeking godly counsel, we felt certain of God's blessing to purchase a summer camp for kids that was situated on three small beautifully wooded lakes just south of Leech Lake near Walker, Minnesota. The previous owners of Camp Fish had built a facility that was, in essence, an angling laboratory combined with a fishing education complex, but after four years they had not been able to make their dream financially viable.

The camp had developed a curriculum that espoused a whole outdoor way of life, instructing kids on how to fish at a very high level as well as acquainting them with the fishing tackle industry

Chapter Eight

Camp Fish and the Fishers of Men

by RON LINDNER

"Come, follow me,"
Jesus said, "and I
will make you fishers
of men."

MATTHEW 4:19

and the basics of aquatic biology. Al and I and some of our In-Fisherman staff volunteered our time as guest speakers and teachers and advisors. For many of the campers (approximately 700 a year), fishing became not just a pastime or a hobby or even a sport, but a *passion!* And a number of them are working in the sport fishing industry today.

By this time the In-Fisherman Communication's Network had grown beyond our magazine to include a syndicated television and radio show as well as "on the water" schools, several books, instructional videos, and traveling seminars. Our mission statement read: "Teaching North America to catch fish is our business," and we *really meant it.* With that vision and commitment, Camp Fish seemed to fit like a glove. And while the work accomplished there with young people is a story that delights my heart, the facility also served another purpose . . . an even higher purpose.

While kids' activities dominated the summer, after Labor Day we ran an outreach at the camp for ten years that became known as the Fishers of Men Retreats. Early autumn in the North Country brings some of the best fishing opportunities of the year, and here we had a facility that could not only house and feed 100 people, but it had large halls and classrooms for lectures and meetings as well. We also had all the equipment to produce a first-class angling experience. And our permanent staff who ran the camp were all Christians.

Prior to buying the camp, I had been meeting with a special group of recovering alcoholics who wanted to go beyond mere lip service to the 12 Steps. My experience with AA is described in the last chapter of this book. At the time the group was focusing on the third step, ". . . made a decision to turn [your] life and [your] will over to the care of God," and

Many men go fishing all of their lives

without knowing that

it is not fish they are after.

HENRY DAVID THOREAU

I knew from personal experience that commitment better be to Jesus Christ. I thought the best way to facilitate this would be to get a group together and fly into a remote Canadian fishing camp. We would spend three intensive days of fishing and soul searching with absolutely no distractions—no TVs, radios, phones—and no way out.

So for this first effort, thirteen "born again" fishermen invited thirteen "searchers for the truth" fishermen. The inviting Christians were asked to pray for their particular guest for the entire week preceding the retreat. Everyone attended a morning session by our evangelist, and then "searchers" were paired with believers to go out in the boats, but not with the person who brought them. The focus was to allow the Holy Spirit to work and speak through our lives while enjoying days of great

"The two best times to fish
is when it's rainin'
and when it ain't."

PATRICK F. McMANUS

fishing. After supper there was another hour or so of explaining the "simple gospel," focusing on God's biblical plan for salvation and that alone. Then we broke into small groups, and questions were encouraged. Many hours of good discussions took place in the solitude around a bonfire and under a beautiful starlit sky.

The last session before everyone flew out, the evangelist asked for those who wanted to turn their life and will over to Jesus to stand up. On that first retreat, everyone did, and many made verbal confessions for Jesus. For the attendees as well as for Al and me and our Christian friends who had come along to speak and give counsel, it lived up to its billing as the "fishing trip of a lifetime"—both for fish and *for men!* (By the way, one guy caught a thirteen-pound walleye!)

This trip was the genesis and model for fifteen Fishers of Men fishing trips that followed. Ten of these retreats were held at Camp Fish, which hosted as many as 100 fishermen. However, we found that if there were more than 70 or 80 attendees, the personal aspects that were so important to these sessions were lost. We also tried to keep a balance of one believer to one searcher for the truth. People of various religious and nonreligious backgrounds were always welcomed, and we trusted completely in the leading of the Holy Spirit to change lives. We relied upon different evangelists as our primary speakers, different people (usually fishing personalities) told their faith stories, and pastors of various churches helped out.

The method of inviting people was unique. Al and I would send invitations to Christian brothers who were avid fishermen, and within their sphere of acquaintances and friends, they in turn would seek out individuals who had been on their heart and who might be open to coming. Consequently, we had folks come from all walks of life—from lawyers to farmers to accountants to salesmen to fishing guides—and from different parts of the country. All slept dormitory style, with wood-burning stoves, bunk beds with sleeping bags, and excessive snoring. Most of the 1,000 men who came loved it.

While the spiritual agenda for the retreat was always made clear, part of the lure was the fishing. Just a chance to fish or talk with Al or the other well-known anglers who were on hand to help out brought many men to the camp. Famous bass tournament anglers such as Shaw Grigsby and Jay Yelas were guest speakers at one retreat. For those whose preference was walleyes, tourney champs Darrell Christianson and Mark Dorn came to give their testimonies and answer questions after sessions. For football fans, Wally Hilgenberg was enlisted as a speaker (he also loves to fish).

After a few of the men's retreats, Mary and Dolores felt led to have a follow-up weekend at Camp Fish for the wives. Many of the men returned home with changed lives, and their wives wanted to know what had happened. Some were even perplexed. The women's sessions were called Sonshine Weekends and usually followed a few weeks after the men's. To accomplish this some of the men stayed home with the kids so their wives could hear the message they had heard, which reflected a monumental change of heart toward their wives. Typically about 60 women would attend these meetings, and for many of the eventual 500 women who came, it was the first chance to hear the "good news."

For the Sonshine Weekends, the ambiance in the camp was transformed from a rough, outdoorsmen hideaway to a very quiet secluded

spot for women to open up and listen to what God might say to them. The agenda for the women's camp mirrored that of the men's camps, with volleyball, hiking, and canoeing being added to the main activity of fishing. Female evangelists did the speaking, and various women gave testimonies. The one requirement for both the men and women was that they attend each and every session.

Three-fourths of the earth's surface is water,

and one-fourth is land.

It is quite clear that the good Lord intended us

to spend triple the amount of time fishing

as taking care of the lawn.

CHUCK CLARK

Al and I along with other men would volunteer to serve the meals and work in the kitchen. Some of the women did the same for the men's retreats. It was in our hearts to offer these weekend retreats at no cost. In fact, the invitation stated they would not be asked to join a church or partake in any ritual, but should simply come with an open mind and listen with their heart. A collection was never taken. The theme of the weekend was that of the Gospel: "the price has already been paid." We were more than rewarded by just being able to be a small part in God's plan to reach people for Jesus.

Countless stories could be told of what happened at these retreats, but one story stands out in particular. An angler who was fishing Leech Lake for the weekend stopped at Camp Fish to get some information. A session was just starting in the main hall, which he thought was a fishing seminar, so he sat down and listened. That night he returned and accepted Jesus into his life. This man has gone on to share the Gospel with many others while fishing in a boat, reminiscent of the apostles who worked the Sea of Galilee. His wife came to faith through him, and in later years both were healed miraculously—one from cancer and the other from congestive heart failure.

The Bible states that "neither he who plants nor he who waters is anything, but only God, who makes things grow" (1 CORINTHIANS 3:7), and we saw this demonstrated over and over at the camp. We watched individuals whose loved ones had prayed for them for years finally surrender to Jesus Christ. Others who had walked away from the faith for a time returned to Him at our retreats. And some left the camp without making a decision, but later contacted us to say thanks for their special weekend and that they had since become Christians. While we never did an actual follow-up, we know that a very high percentage came to faith. And many believers said that the weekends strengthened their walk and moved them to make certain changes in their lives.

Today, one man who came to Christ at the camp is being used mightily by God to build churches in Russia. Another man is a senior member of a large national Christian youth ministry. We had an optometrist accept Jesus and then go on to replicate the retreats in Wisconsin. A chiropractor did the same thing in Ontario, Canada, and continues today. We

know that many men and women were reconciled with their families and are active Christians today, bringing family and friends into the kingdom of God. And as an extra special gift from the Lord to me, one of my sons came to accept Jesus at one of these retreats.

So, given all the wonderful blessings of Camp Fish and the Fishers of Men Retreats, why did I initially express my ultimate frustrations with this venture? "Every good tree bears good fruit" (Matthew 7:18), and this tree obviously bore good fruit. What's my problem?

The frustration was that over the decade we ran Camp Fish, it never came close to breaking even. Despite our love for the camp, nothing we did or tried brought it out of the deep red. We had special sessions for troubled kids, for fathers and sons, parent and child. We started a newsletter called In-Fisher Kids and promoted the camp on TV and

radio and through all our media outlets. We even appealed to the
tackle and boating industries to help out. After ten years, however, in
order for Camp Fish to function at the high level for which it was
originally designed, we realized the only way was to subsidize it per-
petually. The overhead, insurance, taxes, and the short season were
simply too much. But our Board of Directors and financial advisers
told us the In-Fisherman's pockets were simply not deep enough to
bear the ongoing costs. In 1994, to our dismay, we closed Camp Fish
and then sold the grounds.

REFLECTION

by RON LINDNER

After we sold the camp, we held a few more Fishers of Men Retreats in different locations. And in conjunction with the Berkley Line Company, the extensive fishing curriculum and materials we developed for teaching were donated to the U.S. Fish and Wildlife Service and used at sites across the country to instruct kids—parts of which are still in use today.

For me, however, it's still a puzzle. I keep thinking we may have missed God's leading somewhere. Al, Mary, and Dolores feel God simply wanted us to have the camp for a decade, touch the lives we did, and then move on. I hope that's true. We ran the camp as long as we possibly could, trying to be good stewards of what God had given us. For me personally, it was the biggest disappointment in my In-Fisherman career. I've never been back to the grounds since we decided to sell it. I just didn't have the heart.

King Solomon said, "There is a time for everything, and a season for every activity under heaven"(ECCLESIASTES 3:1). *Maybe that was what Camp Fish was, "a season."* ⤚×

Chapter Nine

Angel on the Ice

by AL LINDNER

*But during the night
an angel of the Lord
opened the doors of the jail
and brought them out.*

ACTS 5:19

IT'S BEEN TWENTY YEARS SINCE I COMMITTED MY LIFE TO JESUS CHRIST. I was thirty-seven in June 1982, and one of those statistically rare people who come to faith later in life. Not long after that season of spiritual transformation, I had another experience that changed my life.

In the late afternoon on the day before Thanksgiving, I decided to leave the office early and go home and catch some bluegills for our evening meal. I lived on a small lake just out of Brainerd called Perch Lake that's good for pan fish and bass. In our area of northern Minnesota, Thanksgiving typically marks the first time on the small lakes when you have plenty of safe ice to walk out on (3-4 inches). Our lake had a good 3 inches, and there was no snow cover. It was just a solid sheet of clear ice.

When I got home, I grabbed my bucket of fishing gear, tossed in some wax worms for bait, and picked up my ice chisel. There's a point of land

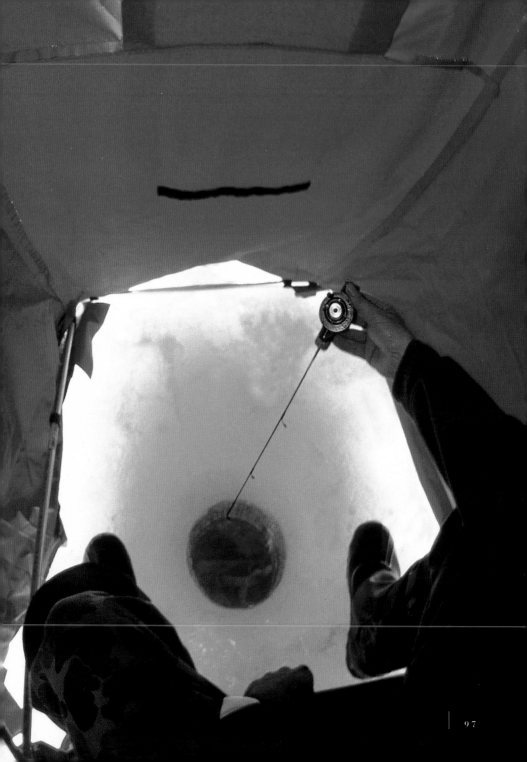

that separates the bay we lived on from another small bay, which was where I usually went for bluegills, crappies, and an occasional bass early in the season. That bay was only about a block away from our property.

I strolled across the ice to my favorite spot and broke a hole through the ice with my chisel. It didn't take long before I started catching fish and had a great time. Both my sons were playing with some of their buddies on the ice, slipping and sliding around me, just having fun. After a while they got cold and tired out and headed to the house, leaving me alone on the ice with my thoughts.

There's something magical about the twilight hours on a lake at this time of year. The flickering sunshine reflects off the ice all around you, and the sunlight falls softly into the hushed seclusion of the lake. I love the long, slanting bars of light that strike the treetops around the edge of the water and the deep shadows on the hills. The trees, though stripped and bare except for a few brown leaves, stand tall and strong to face the cool, bracing air of early winter.

There is certainly

something in angling

that tends to produce

a serenity of the mind.

WASHINGTON IRVING

It was a sight I enjoyed until it was just about dark. The bluegill bite was just about over, and I had plenty of fish to fry. So I tossed my gear into the bucket along with the frozen fish, carried my ice chisel in my right hand, and headed back around the point for home. There was a scent of coming snow in the air, and I was drinking in long, deep breaths of it as I plodded along.

I got to a spot in the bay in front of my house where I know there's a little drop-off in about 8 feet of water, and I suddenly stopped. I had just taken a step forward with my right foot in front, and I paused for a moment with my legs spread in this position and looked down at the ice. There was nothing but silence around me.

Something about the ice looked strange . . . something was different in a way that I'll never be able to describe. So I took my chisel from my right hand, laid it out in front of my right foot, and tapped down to check the ice. In that moment the chisel broke through the ice, and I slipped forward. With the extra weight that went out on my right foot, the ice suddenly cracked without warning.

I went down with it, and I remember plunging forward into the freezing water. Instinctively, I lifted my right arm up because I saw what looked like another piece of ice. It was almost like a hole in the ice. My right arm caught at the elbow on the other end of the ice, and instantly my full weight jerked my right shoulder back really hard, and the back of my shoulder pushed all the way out. It flashed through my mind that I'd just dislocated my shoulder . . . and then everything . . . went . . . blank.

I remember nothing of what happened next . . . nothing. The lights went out, outer silence became inner silence, and I felt nothing.

The next thing I knew I was on my knees on the ice at the edge of the hole. My left hand was supporting my weight on the ice, and my right arm was dangling loose. Soaking wet, I could still feel my shoulder bumped out in the back. I stood up, knowing I was hurt bad, and leaned forward with my right shoulder and felt it roll sickenly back into the socket.

I took a deep breath and gazed around, searching the ice for whoever had gotten me out of the water. But there was no one on the ice but me, and there was no way I had pulled myself out.

Fortunately, it was not a bitterly cold night. I grabbed my bucket of gear and fish, walked back up to the house, and went into the garage. I told Mary what had happened, then went in and got out of my wet clothes. We had a nice fish dinner, and I felt my shoulder really starting to ache. I didn't know how bad it was hurt, though, until I laid down in bed. The pain became unbearable, and I had no choice but to have Mary drive me to the hospital emergency room. They immobilized my arm, gave me some pain killers, which I took in abundance, and with time, praise God, it healed.

Perhaps you believe there's a natural explanation for how I made it home that night, but I can tell you that unless there was an angel walking beside me on Perch Lake I would have been a goner. Angels are said to be "ministering spirits sent to serve those who will inherit salvation" (HEBREWS 1:14), and my angel earned his wings that night. I just wish I could have gotten a peek...even for a second.

SO PETER WAS KEPT IN PRISON, but the church was earnestly praying to God for him. The night before Herod was to bring him to trial, Peter was sleeping between two soldiers, bound with two chains, and sentries stood guard at the entrance. Suddenly an angel of the Lord appeared and a light shone in the cell. He struck Peter on the side and woke him up. "Quick, get up!" he said, and the chains fell off Peter's wrists. Then the angel said to him, "Put on your clothes and sandals." And Peter did so. "Wrap your cloak around you and follow me," the angel told him. Peter followed him out of the prison, but he had no idea that what the angel was doing was really happening; he thought he was seeing a vision. They passed the first and second guards and came to the iron gate leading to the city. It opened for them by itself, and they went through it. When they had walked the length of one street, suddenly the angel left him. Then Peter came to himself and said, "Now I know without a doubt that the Lord sent his angel and rescued me from Herod's clutches and from everything the Jewish people were anticipating." ACTS 12:5-11

REFLECTION

by AL LINDNER

I can't tell you how many times over the past twenty years I have thought about this incident. I'll never forget that fraction of a second when the Holy Spirit warned me that something was wrong, the catching of my elbow and searing pain, then waking from unconsciousness. I believe with all my heart that an angel of God caught me up and set me down on the edge of the ice. The Word of God is filled with stories of angelic intervention, and the psalmist said the Lord "will command his angels concerning you to guard you in all your ways; they will lift you up in their hands..." (PSALM 91:11-12). *I've been in those hands...once, at least, and it's a great place to be.*

MY LOVE FOR FISHING BEGAN AS A YOUNG
CHILD AT MY PARENTS' LAKE CABIN IN
NORTHERN WISCONSIN. It was a great escape
from our big-city life in Chicago, and everything
about the sport fascinated me.

Even after a stint in the army in the early '50s
and over the next twelve years of working in
Chicago, my only dream was to move my family
to lake country. I thought about new lures, new
reels, new lakes, and new fish-catching tech-
niques. Al and I spent our weeknights making
lures in my basement, testing them on weekend
fishing trips, and reading everything we could
find on fishing. I remember telling my wife,
Dolores, that if I could make $10,000 a year and
work in the sport fishing world, I would be the
happiest man in the world!

Chapter Ten

*The End
of the Line*

by RON LINDNER

*The wages of sin is death,
but the gift of God
is eternal life in
Christ Jesus our Lord.*

ROMANS 6:23

In 1965, during Al's tour of military duty in Vietnam, he and I decided to follow our dreams and move "up north" and find our way into the sport fishing business. When he returned in 1966, we moved first to Wisconsin and then to Minnesota, getting our start in the fishing tackle and guide business. Over the next thirteen years, Al and I invented and marketed numerous lures, with some selling in the millions. We launched and later sold Lindy Tackle company, authored many books and articles, fished tournaments, produced radio shows, published a fishing magazine, and aired a nationally syndicated television show.

To capture the fish

is not all of the fishing.

ZANE GREY

Despite our amazing success, happiness eluded me. Something was missing in my life, but I didn't know what it was. During this time, I lived my fantasy of fishing from the Atlantic to the Pacific and from the Arctic to the Caribbean, while my wife was at home raising our seven children without me. I ran with hard-living people, which caught

up with me when I got my third DUI in 1973. My drinking problem forced me to join Alcoholics Anonymous.

For the next five years I struggled with alcohol. I'd stay clean for months, then a night or two of drinking was followed by weeks of guilt, remorse, and depression. While I sincerely did not want to drink, the temptation was unrelenting. And the longer I stayed sober, the more the pressure intensified.

The breaking point came on Good Friday in 1978. After nine months of sobriety, I was driving to the Minneapolis Sports Show, and deep down I knew I was going to drink that weekend. Despite my involvement and training in AA, I walked into the show and went straight to the beer

stand. I literally inhaled the first beer, then another . . . and another throughout the day. After the show closed, I went to a restaurant bar and remember downing several Manhattans before a dark black curtain rolled down over my consciousness . . . and it was lights out.

The next thing I knew I was lying in my hotel room with crumpled, dirty clothes spread around the floor. My head was swimming, I was pouring sweat, and my arm was black and blue. There was $8 on the nightstand, although I remembered bringing over $200 in cash. After taking a quick shower, I hobbled down to the lobby and asked if there

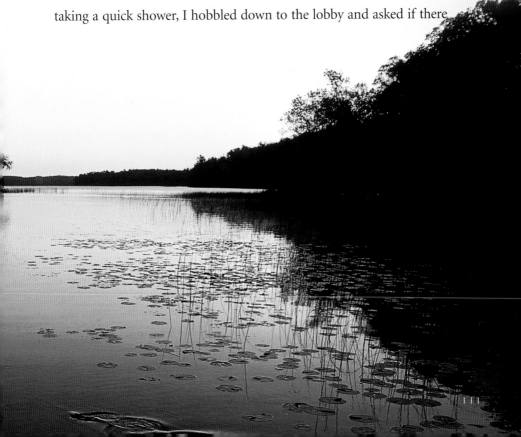

were any messages. The clerk asked if I'd like to check out, but I told him I'd be staying until Sunday. He gave me an odd look and said it was Sunday. Not only had I blacked out, but I had lost an entire day and a half!

When I went out to the parking lot, my car was missing. In a panic, I reported it stolen, only to have the police find it parked two blocks away where I had obviously left it. Later, I learned that I had made a complete fool out of myself at the sports show as well as the restaurant.

Loaded with shame and utter emptiness, I started the three-hour drive back to Brainerd. Flipping through radio stations, I stopped as a preacher quoted from 1 Corinthians 6:9-10. "Do you not know that the wicked will not inherit the kingdom of God? Do not be deceived: Neither the sexually immoral nor idolaters nor adulterers nor male prostitutes nor homosexual offenders nor thieves nor the greedy nor *drunkards* . . ."

That hit me like a ton of bricks. *I was a drunk* . . . a lost, damaged soul. Although I had always believed there was a God, nothing in my life reflected it. I was out of excuses about turning the corner on a better tomorrow.

When I arrived home, I didn't tell Dolores what had happened. But the first thing she said was, "There's an evangelist preaching over in Crosby-Ironton tomorrow, and I'd like to hear him. Do you want to go?"

"Sure," I mumbled, feeling so guilty I would have agreed to anything.

The next evening we went to the little town of Crosby. The evangelist's name was Lowell Lundstrom, and little by little, his words began to meld with the words of the radio preacher. Pointedly, his message came with the conviction of the Holy Spirit that drunkards would never see the kingdom of heaven. I suddenly realized that unless God had an alternate plan for my life, I was at the end of the line.

Then I heard Lundstrom say something about forgiveness and a new life and becoming a new creature. I wasn't sure what all this meant, but I instinctively knew this was the good news I desperately needed! When he asked if anyone wanted to come forward and receive Jesus Christ, I jumped out of my seat and almost ran up to that stage! I stood there, not caring if anyone joined me and not quite sure of what was going on. Soft organ music was playing, and a few others slowly filtered up. To my left an old man was weeping.

All of a sudden I felt a hand grab my arm, and I looked over and it was Dolores. She looked at me and smiled, which melted my hard heart right on the spot.

I don't know how close I'd come to spooling God's reel, but I knew I was close! All the fight was out of me. Lundstrom then led us in a prayer of confessing our sins, asking God to forgive us, and inviting Jesus Christ to come into our lives as Lord and Savior.

It would be months, indeed years, before I fully realized what God did for me at that moment. But the most obvious and incredible change was a complete freedom from alcoholism! With the gentle net of His grace, He had scooped me into His boat. And this was not catch and release. He put me into His live well of eternal life . . . *forever!*

REFLECTION

by RON LINDNER

Looking back on my life, the biggest snag to my finding true happiness came from a total misunderstanding of God's love and grace. It took a blackout weekend in Minneapolis to bring me to the place where I understood that salvation is a gift of God that comes to us by faith. We can never earn or merit it. We simply need to believe the truth that Jesus Christ gave His life and blood to forgive us our sins. It is that easy!

Perhaps you have run out of tomorrows and pulled yourself to the end of the line. If you want to find peace with God, the Bible states "that if you confess with your mouth, 'Jesus is Lord,' and believe in your heart that God raised him from the dead, you will be saved" (ROMANS 10:9). *If you want to receive Jesus Christ into your life today, He will come in and change you in ways you never imagined.* ⤫

Chapter Eleven

One Last Cast

by RON LINDNER

Jesus answered, "I tell you the truth, no one can enter the kingdom of God unless he is born of water and the Spirit.... You should not be surprised at my saying, 'You must be born again.'"

JOHN 3:5, 7

AL AND I HAVE LIVED MOST OF OUR LIVES DOING WHAT WE LOVE TO DO, AND FISHING HAS NEVER GROWN OLD. When it's first light on the water, we want to be there, and at the end of the day, it's still hard to take that "one last cast." I'd like a nickel for every cast I made after my "just one more cast" for the day.

Before we close this book, we'd like to take one last cast in your direction. You've read our faith stories, and some of the ways our faith has influenced the decisions we've had to make along life's road. Al and I are both "born again Christians," and it's possible that you're not certain what that means.

Over the years, I realize the term "born again Christian" has developed some negative connotations. Today, some say the term is an oxymoron—

"You will find angling to be like the virtue of humility,

which has a calmness of spirit

and a world of other blessings attending upon it."

SIR IZAAK WALTON, *The Compleat Angler*

meaning that if you call yourself a Christian, you must automatically be "born again," and nothing else is necessary. Others point to the negative, unloving actions of someone who calls himself or herself "born again," and they conclude that the words are meaningless. And for many people, the term has been so misused that it has become just another tired religious cliché.

Game fish
are too valuable
to be caught only once.
LEE WULFF

For much of our lives, Al and I were no different than most people when it comes to spiritual things. It wasn't that we didn't believe in God. It's just that we didn't care that much. Spiritual words such as "born again" had little meaning either way—negatively or positively. We simply didn't understand. But as you've read, that all changed for both of us, and that "new birth" changed our lives and our families.

When Jesus spoke the words, "You must be born again," to Nicodemus in the third chapter of the gospel of John, it was a direct, uncompromising statement. Jesus did not offer those words as simply a good idea, or a nice suggestion, and something you might consider as an option or alternative to something else. Nicodemus was already a deeply religious man, among the national leadership of Pharisees in the Sanhedrin, the supreme council of the Jews, so it wasn't about becoming more religious. Nicodemus was already stuffed to the gills with religion. Jesus said that to enter the Kingdom of God one must first have his or her heart changed, which Nicodemus . . . and I . . . struggled to understand.

You've read my personal account of how God intervened in my life after a drunken blackout weekend in Minneapolis. When I heard those words that had first been spoken to Nicodemus, "You must be born again," I did not understand how God could do that in my life. But I was at the end of my line, and I finally understood that I must do things His way to find peace, serenity, and joy. It would only be later . . . after I surrendered my life and will over to the care of Jesus Christ as my personal Savior that I came to understand it.

Since that time, I've heard many euphemisms used to explain the process of salvation: "Making Jesus Lord of your life," "accepting Jesus as your personal Savior," "coming to the cross," "making a decision for Christ," "having a personal relationship with Jesus," "confessing Christ as Lord," and the list goes on and on. Still, the process of being "born again," no matter what it's called, comes down to this: we acknowledge that we are sinners; we repent or turn away from our sins; we accept Jesus' death on the cross as the only means to our forgiveness and receive a washing away of our sins through the blood of Christ; and we ask Jesus to come into our hearts through the Holy Spirit and make us a new person.

If you are at the end of some line in your life or are moved to seek peace for your soul, you can pray this simple prayer that I learned many years ago: "Father, I am a sinner, and I'm sorry for the sins in my life. I ask you to forgive me and to cleanse my heart with the blood of your Son Jesus. I give you my life. Jesus, come into my heart as Lord and Savior, and

direct my paths by the Holy Spirit from this day forward. Thank you for giving Your life for me, and help me to always live for you. Amen."

This is certainly not the end of the matter. It is, in fact, only the beginning—the beginning of a life in a personal relationship with God. Where will it lead? Well, ultimately into the eternal Kingdom of God—just as Jesus told Nicodemus it would. But in the meantime, along the way, wherever God leads you, I guarantee that it will be the most exciting, exhilarating, and satisfying portion of your whole life.

REFLECTION

by AL LINDNER

Wherever Jesus Christ went it was reported that "the blind receive sight, the lame walk, those who have leprosy are cured, the deaf hear, the dead are raised, and the good news is preached to the poor" (MATTHEW 11:5). *The blind opened their eyes for the first time . . . and saw their God. The ears of the deaf were healed, and the first sound they heard was the voice of Jesus Christ. The lame man sprang up from the dust and walked and leapt and praised God, and was judged a fool by those who had never known such joy. Those who had never spoken suddenly broke a lifetime of silence with songs of praise.*

When the grace of God came into Ron's life and into my heart and made us new men, it removed the spiritual blindness, deafness, and brokenness of our lives. It was an infinite task, and could only be accomplished by God, but amazing grace had its way with us; and today there is no condemnation for those who are in Christ Jesus. We can say in truth, "All those old things have passed away, and all things have become new, and we are more than conquerors through Him who loves us."

Today there are many new philosophies, new revelations, new ways of trying to please God or "gods," and I see people chasing after them to try to seize this or that promise . . . only to return hungrier and thirstier than ever. Don't go that way. True faith in Christ will deliver you from any emptiness. Grace will be poured into your heart; delivering mercy shall be the anchor of your life.

If you have Christ in your heart, then real life is possible, joy is possible, peace is possible, under all circumstances and in all places. Everything that your soul can desire, it possesses. Those who have Christ in their hearts have the "rivers of life" flowing in them that never fails.   ☧

Estelle and Art Lindner,
Al and Ron's parents

The Next
Generation

In-Fisherman
25th Anniversary

THE JOURNAL OF FRESHWATER FISHING

SPECIAL ISSUE

America's angling
legends talk fishing 2000.

Al Lindner, Ray Scott &
Johnny Morris: Mil...

Doug Hannon ✦ Ron Lin...
Cabela ✦ Dick Pearson ✦
Petros ✦ Buck Perry ✦
Martin ✦ Billy Westmor...
Thill ✦ Larry Dahlberg ✦
Circle ✦ Mark Sa...
Houston ✦ Bill...
Gary Roach...
schde ✦...
Doug...
itch T...
The B...

LEFT: The Millenium Men, Ray, Johnny & Al,
In-Fisherman, March 2000
CENTER: Ron reading to Al at cabin
on Grindstone Lake, Wisconsin
RIGHT: Al with first fish caught off
Ron's deck on Gull Lake, Minnesota

Great is the LORD and most worthy of praise;
    his greatness no one can fathom.
One generation will commend your works to another;
    they will tell of your mighty acts.
They will speak of the glorious splendor of your majesty,
    and I will meditate on your wonderful works.
They will tell of the power of your awesome works,
    and I will proclaim your great deeds.
They will celebrate your abundant goodness
    and joyfully sing of your righteousness.

PSALM 145:3-7

Art Lindner (left)
with Ron and Ron's
boy, Billy

LEFT TO RIGHT:
Ron's daughter, Dawn Lindner,
and granddaughter, Elizabeth,
Catch Magazine, 2003.
Al's son, Troy Lindner,
Outdoor Life, May 2002.
Ron and Al,
North American Fisherman 2003.
Ron's son, Daniel Lindner,
Salt Water Sportsman, September 1999.

Unleash Your Greatness

AT BRONZE BOW PUBLISHING WE ARE COMMITTED to helping you achieve your ultimate potential in functional athletic strength, fitness, natural muscular development, and all-around superb health and youthfulness.

HOW TO *feel great* ALL THE TIME

A LIFELONG PLAN for UNLIMITED ENERGY and RADIANT GOOD HEALTH

Newly REVISED and UPDATED

VALERIE SAXION

feel great ALL THE TIME

How to Detoxify & Renew Your Body From Within

VALERIE SAXION

feel great ALL THE TIME

How to Stop Candida & Other Yeast Conditions in Their ...

VALERIE SAXION

feel great ALL THE TIME

The Easy Way to Regain & Maintain ...r Perfect ...eight

...LERIE ...XION

feel great ALL THE TIME

Conquering the Fatigue, Depression, & Weight Gain Caused by Low Thyroid

VALERIE SAXION

feel great ALL THE TIME

Super Foods for Super Kids and everyone else too!

35 Nutritious, Delicious Meals to Introduce Your Child to a Lifetime of Vibrant Health

VALERIE SAXION, N.D.

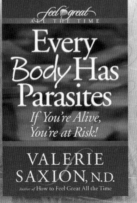

feel great ALL THE TIME

Every Body Has Parasites

If You're Alive, You're at Risk!

VALERIE SAXION, N.D.

Author of How to Feel Great All the Time

NAVY SEAL BREAKTHROUGH TO MASTER LEVEL FITNESS

The Ultimate Training System to Incredible Strength & a Body-to-Die-For

MARK De LISLE

OUR BOOKS, VIDEOS, NEWSLETTERS, Web sites, and training seminars will bring you the very latest in scientifically validated information that has been carefully extracted and compiled from leading scientific, medical, health, nutritional, and fitness journals worldwide.

Our goal is to empower you! To arm you with the best possible knowledge in all facets of strength and personal development so that you can make the right choices that are appropriate for *you*.

Now, as always, **the difference between greatness and mediocrity** begins with a choice. It is said that knowledge is power. But that statement is a half truth. Knowledge is power only when it has been tested, proven, and applied to your life. At that point knowledge becomes wisdom, and in wisdom there truly is *power*. The power to help you choose wisely.

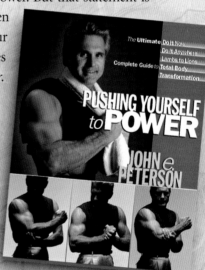

So join us as we bring you the finest in health-building information and natural strength-training strategies to help you reach your ultimate potential.

For information on all our exciting new sports and fitness products, contact:

BRONZE BOW PUBLISHING
2600 East 26th Street
Minneapolis, Minnesota 55406
612.724.8200
TOLL FREE **866.724.8200**
FAX **612.728.8995**

WEB SITES / www.bronzebowpublishing.com / www.masterlevelfitness.com